# CONTENTS

Copyright © 2026 Amelia May Summers

All rights reserved

The characters and events portrayed in this book are fictitious. Any similarity to real persons, living or dead, is coincidental and not intended by the author.

No part of this book may be reproduced, or stored in a retrieval system, or transmitted in any form or by any means, electronic, mechanical, photocopying, recording, or otherwise, without express written permission of the publisher.

ISBN-979-8-9945650-7-0

Cover design by: Amelia May Summers
Library of Congress Control Number: 2026911550
Printed in the United States of America

*Dedication:*

*To my dad, the lightning bolt who worried through every problem until he found the perfect fix, and who taught me that love is shown in the pauses, the calls, and the care. Every day, I feel the quiet ache of missing you, yet your love still guides me.*

*To my family, you are my living legacy, the heartbeat of this book, and the reason every word matters so deeply. Though I am far from perfect, I have tried my best, pouring my heart and soul into loving each of you. You showed me what it means to truly love, to show up, to hold space, and to make someone feel seen, cherished, and valued every single day. I love each and every one of you.- S.W.A.K.*

*To my husband, the one person in this world with whom I have always felt truly safe to be myself, every imperfect, messy, beautiful part. You are the steady presence that has held me through every season, the gentle mirror that has shown me my own worth when I couldn't see it. Through your unwavering love, you taught me how to love myself, deeply, kindly, and without apology. And together, in the quiet miracle of our shared life, we brought our children into the world, and through them came the gift of our beautiful grandchildren, the living bridge between generations, the loves of our life, carrying forward the heartbeat of our family in ways we never could have dreamed. They are the beautiful proof of generational love: one chapter flowing into the next, each generation richer because of the love we planted together. You are my true love, my soulmate, the foundation beneath every joy we've built, every memory we've made, and every future we're still dreaming as a family across the years. Thank you for being my safe place, my greatest teacher, my forever home, and the one who helped create this unbroken chain of love that spans generations. I love you-always.*

*To every heart reading this book, may the warm, steady legacy you are already building continue to grow in the hearts of your loved ones, carrying forward the love you give so beautifully every day.*

*With all my heart,*
*Amelia-Oma (Grandma)*

# INTRODUCTION: WHY LEGACY MATTERS MORE THAN YOU MAY THINK

Imagine this: You're 85, sitting on a porch swing, the sun setting behind you.
Your children and grandchildren are laughing inside.
Someone asks, "What are you most proud of?"
You don't mention the house, the savings, or the titles you held.
You say, "I made them feel loved. Every single one of them knew, deep down, that they mattered to me."

That's legacy.
Not a bank account. Not a resume. Not a trophy case.
Legacy is the way people feel when they think of you.
The warmth that lingers after you're gone.
The certainty in their hearts that they were seen, cherished, and valued without a doubt.
Today, the world is louder, faster, more disconnected than ever.
Loneliness is an epidemic.
Yet the antidote has always been the same: intentional, everyday love.

This guide isn't about perfection.
It's about presence.

It's about small, consistent choices that compound into something unbreakable.
My dad taught me this.
He worried over every problem like it was his personal mission.
He'd lose sleep, pace the kitchen, call me at odd hours with "I've got it, here's how to fix that faucet."
But it was never really about the faucet.
It was about saying, "You're important to me. I'm here."
Those calls, those lingering hugs, those quiet "I'm proud of you" moments, that's what lives on.

This book is your invitation to build that kind of legacy.
Through stories, reflections, science-backed insights, and 20 practical challenges, you'll learn how to make the people you love feel truly seen, cherished, and valued.

With a few small, intentional shifts, you can nurture deeper bonds and create a legacy of love that feels warm and lasting.

# A COZY NOTE BEFORE YOU BEGIN

As you hold this book in your hands (or open the e-book on your screen), take a slow, deep breath.

This isn't a book to rush through.
It's not a checklist to finish or a race to the end.

It's a quiet companion for the journey you're already on, the one of building and deepening the legacy of love you're living every day.

Before you turn the next page, I invite you to gather a few simple things, if you can:

- A notebook or journal, something that feels special to you
- A favorite pen that glides easily across the paper
- A few sheets of loose-leaf paper or stationery
- An envelope or two, tucked somewhere close
- Anything that helps you relax: a candle, your favorite blanket, a cherished photo of loved ones, soft music playing in the background, whatever brings you comfort and presence

These aren't requirements.

They're gentle tools to help you pause, reflect, and let the words of your heart find a place to land.

Throughout these pages, you'll find reflection prompts that invite you to linger with a memory, a feeling, or a quiet question.

You'll meet challenges that invite you to act with intention: sometimes writing a letter, sometimes sharing a story, sometimes simply sitting in presence with someone you love.

When those moments arrive, set the book down for a little while.
Pick up your pen.
Let the thoughts flow without hurry.
Write what feels true, even if it's messy or incomplete.
Seal a letter if one is meant to be sent
later.
Savor the quiet as you do it.
This is your space. Your pace. Your legacy of love.

There is no deadline. No perfect way to do this. Only the beautiful, unfolding way that is yours alone.
When you're ready, turn the page.
I'll be right here with you, walking slowly with an open heart, celebrating every step you take to help the people you love feel truly seen, cherished, and valued.

With warmth and gratitude for the love you're already giving, -*Amelia*

# CHAPTER 1: THE POWER OF BEING SEEN

We all have a deep, natural need to be truly noticed. Not just looked at, but really seen and understood. Think about a time someone completely ignored you.
You waved hello across a room and they looked right past you.
Or you shared something exciting and they brushed it off.
It hurts a little, doesn't it?
It can make you feel small or invisible.

Now remember the opposite.
Someone looked straight into your eyes, really listened, and responded with care.
"That sounds tough, I'm here for you" or "That's amazing, tell me more."
Suddenly everything feels different.
You feel connected, valued, and safe.
That moment is powerful.

Psychologist John Gottman, who studied thousands of couples over many years, discovered something simple but life-changing.
The strongest relationships aren't built on perfect communication, shared hobbies, or even romance.
They're built on how often partners respond to each other's little "reaches" for connection.

These "reaches" are everyday moments when someone tries to get your attention or share something with you:

- "l had a rough day at work."
- "I'm nervous about tomorrow."
- "Look at this funny thing I just saw!"

When we respond with kindness, making eye contact, asking a question, giving a gentle touch, or just saying "Tell me more," we're quietly saying: "You matter to me. I see you. I care."

When we miss or ignore those moments, turning away, half-listening, or brushing them off, the connection slowly fades.

Over time, those small missed opportunities add up, creating distance, loneliness, and the quiet feeling that "l don't really matter here."

**Something I've Learned:**

Being truly seen is the foundation of every meaningful relationship and the heart of a lasting legacy.
People remember how you made them feel far more than what you said or gave them.
Every time you pause to notice someone, listen fully, and respond with care, you're giving them the gift of feeling valued.
That gift becomes part of the love and connection they carry for the rest of their lives.

It's simple, but it's powerful: *the smallest moments of attention and presence build the strongest, most enduring bonds.*

**Story:**

My grandmother had this quiet magic about her.
Every time I stepped through her door, she'd pause whatever she was doing, turn to me, look me right in the eyes, and say, "There's

my favorite girl."
I was one of five grandkids, but in that small, still moment, I felt like I was the only one who mattered in the whole world.
That simple habit left a warm spot in my heart that's still there today.
Sometimes all it takes is pausing the rush of life just long enough to really see the person standing there.
And letting them know, right then and there, that they're the most important one in the room.

**Reflection Prompt:**

Who in your life feels truly seen by you right now?
Who might feel invisible?
Write their names.
What one thing could you do tomorrow to change that?

**Challenge 1:**

Today, give someone your full attention for at least 5 minutes.
No phone, no multitasking.
Listen.
Reflect back what they said: "It sounds like you're really excited about that."
Watch how their posture changes when they feel seen.
Note how it makes you feel too, connected, alive.

# CHAPTER 2: CHERISHING THE EVERYDAY MOMENTS

Legacy isn't built in big events like weddings or graduations. It's woven into the ordinary days, the ones that blur together until they're gone.
The Tuesday night dinner where you share a laugh over burnt toast.
The quick text: "Saw this meme and thought of you."
The way you pause to really listen when someone says, "I'm okay" but their voice cracks a little.
These micro-moments compound, like interest in a bank account of love.

Research from the Greater Good Science Center at UC Berkeley shows that small acts of kindness release oxytocin (the "bonding hormone") in both giver and receiver.
This strengthens relationships over time.
Over years, these acts create a safety net of connection that holds people up when life gets hard.

My dad's habit was the phone call.
He'd ring with "I was thinking about that leaky faucet again..."
But really, he was saying, "You're on my mind. You're not alone in this world."
His worry wasn't a flaw; it was his way of showing care.
Those calls weren't dramatic, but they made me feel grounded, cherished in the midst of chaos.

What if we treated the everyday as sacred?
What if we showed up for the mundane with the same energy we bring to holidays?

**Something I've Learned:**

Everyday love is the strongest love.
It doesn't demand grand gestures; it just requires intention and consistency.

**Story:**

Every Tuesday evening, without fail, my dad would call around 6:30 p.m. sharp.
It wasn't planned as a big tradition; it just happened one week when I was newly married, living an hour away, and trying to figure out how to balance work, a new home, and the quiet ache of missing home.
He'd say the same thing every time: "Hey, kiddo, what's for dinner?"
I'd laugh and tell him burnt toast and scrambled eggs on the nights I was too tired, or pasta and sauce from a jar when I hadn't gone grocery shopping.
He never judged.
He'd listen, then tell me about his day: the same old stories about the neighbor's dog, the weather, how the car was acting up again.
Nothing dramatic. Nothing flashy.
Just the steady rhythm of checking in, sharing the ordinary, making sure I knew I wasn't alone in the blur of adult life.

One Tuesday, I was having a rough week, exhausted, overwhelmed, feeling like I was failing at everything.
I answered the phone and tried to sound normal, but my voice cracked when he asked, "You okay?"
I told him I wasn't.

I told him about the pressure, the tiredness, the fear that I wasn't doing any of this right.
He didn't try to fix it.
He didn't give advice.
He just listened, then said, "I know it feels heavy right now. But you're doing better than you think. And I'm proud of you, *burnt toast and all.*"
I cried.
Not loud, dramatic sobs, just quiet tears while he stayed on the line, breathing steady, letting me feel whatever I needed to feel.
When I finally said, "Thanks, Dad," he replied, "Anytime, kiddo. See you next Tuesday."

Those calls continued for years.
They never got longer than fifteen minutes.
They never involved deep life advice or big revelations.
But they were there, week after week, Tuesday after Tuesday, like a heartbeat I could count on when everything else felt unsteady.

Now, years later, I find myself calling my own grown kids on Tuesdays.
Sometimes they're busy, sometimes they're tired, sometimes they're just okay.
But I ask the same question: "Hey, what's for dinner?"
And I listen.
I let them share the burnt toast days, the good days, the hard days.
I tell them I'm proud of them, *burnt toast and all.*

Those ordinary Tuesday nights were never big events.
They were just phone calls.
But they wove us together, thread by thread, into something unbreakable.
They taught me that legacy isn't built in weddings or graduations.

It's built in the quiet, repeated moments, the ones that blur together until they're gone, but leave behind a safety net of love that holds us up when life gets hard.
And that net is still there, catching me, catching them, catching the next generation because one man decided that checking in on a Tuesday mattered more than anything else.

**Reflection Prompt:**

List three everyday moments from last week where you could have cherished someone more.
What stopped you?
How can you show up differently next time?

**Challenge 2:**

Create one simple, everyday ritual this month, something small, meaningful, and easy to repeat daily (or once a week if daily feels too ambitious at first).
Examples:

- A quick morning text to your child sharing one thing you're grateful for about them
- A goodnight phone call or voice message to a parent
- A shared 10-minute coffee break with your partner, phone-free, just to connect

Choose one that feels doable and heartfelt.

Commit to it for the full month, every day if possible, or the same day each week (like every Sunday evening).

To hold yourself gently accountable, write it down right now: In your journal, notebook, or even a note on your phone, record:

- The exact ritual you're choosing
- How often you'll do it (daily or specific day(s) of the week)
- When you'll start (e.g., tomorrow morning)
- A short reason why it matters to you and your loved ones

Seeing it written in your own words makes it real.
It becomes a quiet promise to yourself and to the people you love.

Start small. Stay consistent.
Watch how this one tiny thread, woven day by day or week by week, slowly strengthens the whole fabric of your relationships, one loving knot at a time.

## Bonus: Daily Moments of Love and Connection

**Guidance for this page:**

Use this tracker for one month (or as long as feels right). Each evening, spend just 2-3 minutes reflecting on the day. Jot quick notes-no need for essays. The goal is awareness and celebration of small moments of love.

**Layout:**

Day of the week/ small act of love / how it made someone feel (or how I felt giving it)/ one thing I'm grateful for in our connection

**Example:**

Monday / 20-second hug before school / Their smile melted my heart / The way their little arms squeezed back so tightly

**Week 1-Dates:**
Mon:
Tue:
Wed:
Thu:
Fri:
Sat:
Sun:

**Week 2-Dates:**
Mon:
Tue:
Wed:
Thu:
Fri:
Sat:
Sun:

**Week 3-Dates:**
Mon:
Tue:
Wed:
Thu:
Fri:
Sat:
Sun:

**Week 4-Dates:**
Mon:
Tue:

Wed:
Thu:
Fri:
Sat:
Sun:

**End-of-Month Reflection:**

1. What patterns do you notice in the ways you showed love?

2. Which moments made your loved ones (or you) feel most seen/ cherished?

3. One new ritual or habit you'd like to carry forward:

4. A note of kindness to yourself: You showed up with love this month, how does that feel?

Remember: This isn't about doing more, it's about noticing the love already present. Your quiet, consistent efforts are weaving the threads of an enduring legacy.

# CHAPTER 3: LETTING THEM KNOW THEY'RE DEEPLY VALUED

Value isn't a feeling you give once and forget. It's a message you repeat through actions, words, and choices, a constant reminder that "You are important to me."

Harvard's 85-year Grant Study, the longest on adult development, found one clear conclusion: "Close relationships and social connections keep us happier and healthier. Period."

People who felt valued lived longer, healthier lives.

So how do you let someone know they are deeply valued?

- Remember small details: "You mentioned loving that book - I got it for you."
- Show up when it matters: Not just birthdays, but the bad days too.
- Celebrate their wins as if they were yours: "I'm so proud- tell me everything!"
- Forgive their mistakes with grace: "We all mess up. I still love you."

**Something I've Learned:**

When people feel valued, they bloom.
And that bloom becomes part of your legacy, a garden of rela-

tionships you nurtured.

**Story:**

My friend Mark, a 34-year-old working dad of one-year-old twins, once shared a story about his own father.
His dad was a man of few words; he never once said "I love you" aloud.
Yet every Saturday morning, while Mark slept in after a long week, his father would drive across town and quietly mow Mark's lawn.
Row after row, he pushed the old mower across the yard, sweat on his brow, giving Mark the precious gift of rest.

No fanfare, no expectation of thanks, just the steady hum drifting through the window, silently saying, "Your rest matters to me. You're worth the effort."
Mark never thanked him properly before his dad passed, but now, as he mows his own lawn while his twins sleep, he understands.

That quiet act wasn't just yard work; it was love in motion, a legacy of care that still echoes in his heart and shapes the father he's become.

Value is often quiet, but it resonates deeply and lasts forever.

**Reflection Prompt:**
Remember a time when you truly felt valued by another person. What specific thing did they do or say?
How can you do the same for others to let them know how deeply they matter to you?

**Challenge 3:**

Write a short "You Matter Because..." note to someone.
Be specific: "You matter because your laugh lights up the room, and you always know how to make me smile on tough days."

Seal it. Give it in person or mail it.

The impact will last longer than you think, and it might just inspire them to pass it on.

# CHAPTER 4: HUGS THAT LINGER - THE PHYSICAL LANGUAGE OF LOVE

Touch is more than skin deep, it's a language of the soul.

In a world that often feels hurried and distant, a simple embrace can become a lifeline.
Science quietly confirms what many of us have always known intuitively: a hug lasting twenty seconds or longer releases a gentle flood of oxytocin, the
"bonding hormone", while significantly lowering cortisol, the stress hormone that so easily builds up inside us.

In a time when studies show many adults go days, even weeks, without meaningful physical contact, your arms can offer something profoundly healing.

Think about what a hug truly says, without needing a single word:
"You're safe here."
"You're not alone."
"You are cherished, exactly as you are."

The warmth lingers long after the arms release.
It settles into the body like a quiet promise, a reminder that connection is still possible, that love can be felt as much as it can be heard.

**Something I've Learned:**

Physical affection builds emotional resilience, for both the giver and the receiver.
It is one of the simplest, most powerful ways to show love that words sometimes struggle to express.

A hug, a hand on the shoulder, a forehead kiss, these small gestures weave safety, trust, and belonging into the very fabric of a relationship, creating memories that the heart never forgets.

**Story:**

My grandma was the undisputed hugger in our family.
From the time I was small enough to disappear into her arms, she had a way of wrapping you up that felt like the world could pause for a moment.

Her hugs weren't quick or obligatory.
She held on, long enough for you to relax, long enough for the tension in your shoulders to soften, long enough for you to feel the steady rhythm of her breathing and know that everything would be okay.

Even as kids, we understood her hugs were different.
They weren't just greetings; they were protection.
A scraped knee, a hard day at school, a worry you couldn't name, she would pull you close, hold you there, and let the quiet safety of her arms do the healing.
Nothing bad could touch you while you were in that embrace.

Years after she passed, I still carry the echo of those hugs.
On days when the world feels too heavy, when grief or stress presses in, I close my eyes and remember the way she held me, like nothing could get through, like I was completely and utterly safe.

That memory alone can steady my breathing, soften my heart, and remind me that love can be felt in the body long after it is

spoken.
Her hugs taught me something I carry into every relationship now: sometimes the most powerful thing we can do is simply hold someone a little longer, letting them feel the steadiness, the warmth, the unspoken promise that "I've got you."

If you're not naturally affectionate, that's okay.
Start small.

- A hand resting gently on a shoulder during a conversation.
- A high-five that lingers a second longer than usual.
- A forehead kiss when saying goodnight.
- A back rub when someone looks tired.

These small touches are doorways, gentle invitations for connection that don't demand anything in return.

**Reflection Prompt:**

Take a slow breath and remember:
When was the last time you gave or received a truly meaningful hug or touch?
How did it feel in your body, the warmth, the safety, the quiet relief?
Who in your life might be longing for that kind of connection right now?
What would it look like to offer it, even in the smallest way?

**Challenge 4:**

Today, offer one intentional moment of physical connection.
It could be a full hug, hold it for at least twenty seconds, long enough to let the warmth settle in.
If hugging isn't comfortable yet, try a long hand-hold, a gentle shoulder squeeze, or a back rub that lingers.

Let the other person feel the steadiness, the presence, the love made tangible through touch.

Afterward, notice the difference: the way the room feels softer, the way your own heart feels fuller, the way the bond between you deepens just a little more.

This is love made real, simple, wordless, and profoundly powerful.
In a world that often forgets how to touch with care, your embrace can become a gift they carry long after the moment has passed.

# CHAPTER 5: THE "JUST CALLING TO SAY HI" REVOLUTION

In our fast-moving world, we text more than we talk. Emails arrive in a constant stream, notifications chime endlessly, and messages stack up like unread mail.
But actual voices? They're growing quieter, rarer, almost forgotten in the noise.
Yet nothing quite replaces the warmth of hearing someone's tone, their familiar laugh, or the gentle pause that carries more meaning than any emoji ever could.

A simple "just calling to say hi" has become a small but powerful act of rebellion against the distance we so easily let creep in.
It whispers, without fanfare:
"l thought of you out of the blue."
"You're worth my time, no agenda, no rush."
"I'm not waiting for a crisis or a holiday to reach out. You matter to me right now."

In a time when it's so easy to stay connected on the surface, choosing to pick up the phone and let your voice reach someone is a quiet, intentional way of saying, "You are important to me, today and always."

Those few minutes on the line can become the threads that hold relationships together through every season of life, through busy weeks, hard months, joyful years, and everything in between.

**Something I've Learned:**

Spontaneous connection fights loneliness. A recent Gallup poll showed that 1 in 3 adults feels lonely regularly, even when surrounded by people. Your call could be the antidote, a small spark that reminds someone they're not invisible, that they're remembered, that they're loved in the ordinary moments of an ordinary day. Those brief, intentional reaches build the strongest bridges.

**Story:**

My best friend Jennifer and I have known each other since college, nearly thirty years of shared laughter, late-night talks, and the kind of friendship that survives moves, marriages, and raising kids.

When the pandemic hit, everything changed.
We couldn't see each other, couldn't hug, couldn't even sit across a table.
The isolation felt endless, and the fear of drifting apart crept in quietly.
One afternoon, feeling particularly alone, I picked up the phone and called her.
No big reason, no crisis, no plan.
Just "Hey... I was thinking about you. How's your heart today?"

She answered, and we talked for maybe five minutes.
She told me about a funny thing her toddler did, I shared a silly work story, we laughed until we cried.
Nothing profound. Nothing that would make headlines.
But when we hung up, something shifted.
The loneliness lifted, just a little.
The next week, she called me.

Then I called her again.
It became our thing: "hi calls."
No agenda, no pressure, just a voice on the other end saying, "I'm here. You're not alone."

Those five-minute chats carried us through the hardest months.

They reminded us that friendship doesn't need big events to survive, it needs presence.

When the world opened up again, we didn't stop.
Even now, years later, with full lives and full calendars, one of us will pick up the phone on a random Wednesday, and the other will answer.
We still laugh, still share the small things, still feel the steadiness of knowing someone is thinking of us in the middle of their day.

That simple habit, those "just calling to say hi" moments, became our lifeline.
It's not dramatic.
It's not a grand gesture.
But it's ours.
And in every call, I hear the quiet promise: "You matter to me, today and always."

That promise is the legacy we're building, one voice, one laugh, one ordinary afternoon at a time.

**Reflection Prompt:**

Take a slow breath and let your mind wander gently to the people in your life right now.
Picture their faces, hear their voices, remember the way they smile or the little things that make them unique.
Who among them would light up, truly brighten, if your name appeared on their phone screen right now?

Who might be having an ordinary, quiet day that could turn warmer with just a few minutes of your voice?
Who have you been meaning to reach out to, even though life keeps pulling you in other directions?

Now, ask yourself honestly:
What's holding you back from calling them in this very moment?
Is it busyness? Worry that it's "not the right time"? Fear they're too occupied? Or simply the habit of letting texts and silence fill the space where a voice could be?

There's no judgment here, only gentle awareness.
Whatever the answer, let it sit with you.
Then imagine how it might feel, for both of you, if you made that call today, tomorrow, or sometime this week.
What small ripple of joy, comfort, or connection could it create?

**Challenge 5:**

This week, create a simple, recurring habit that brings your voice back into the lives of people you care about.
Set a reminder on your phone, twice a week (maybe Tuesday and Friday, or whatever days feel natural to you), labeled something warm like:
"Just say hi"
"Thinking of you call"
"Quick connection moment"

When the reminder pops up, pause whatever you're doing, take a breath, and pick up the phone.
Call someone, no agenda, no big reason needed.
Keep it light and short, under five minutes is perfect.
Just let your voice reach them:
"Hey, I was thinking of you... how's your
day going?"
Or simply: "I just wanted to hear your voice

for a minute." No pressure to talk about
anything deep.
No need to solve problems.
Just presence.
A laugh, a quick update, a shared memory, or even comfortable silence.

Do this twice a week for the next month, and watch what happens.
You may be surprised by how quickly those few minutes strengthen bonds, ease isolation, and bring unexpected joy, not just to them, but to you.

These calls are small, but they are mighty.
They become threads of connection that hold relationships steady through busy seasons, hard days, and ordinary life.
They remind the people you love, and remind you, that you matter to each other, right here, right now.

Your voice is a gift.
Let it be heard.

# CHAPTER 6: WHY MONEY ISN'T THE LEGACY (AND WHAT IS)

At the very end of life, when the room grows quiet and time is short, most people don't speak of bank accounts, titles, possessions, or achievements.
They don't tally savings or recount promotions.

Instead, the words that rise, often in soft whispers, are these:
"I wish I'd spent more time with the people I love."
"I wish I'd told them how much they meant to me."
"I wish I'd been there, really there for them."

These regrets are not about what was earned or accumulated.
They are about what was given, or not given, in the everyday moments of presence, attention, and care.
Money is a tool.
It brings security, comfort, opportunities, and freedom.
It can open doors, fund education, create stability, and ease burdens.
We need it, and planning for it is wise.
But money alone cannot build a legacy that lives on in hearts.
It can buy things, houses, cars, vacations, even shared experiences, but it cannot buy the feeling of being truly seen, cherished, and valued.

Legacy is the emotional imprint you leave behind.
It's the way someone's face softens when they remember your laugh.

It's the comfort they feel recalling your steady presence on a hard day.
It's the quiet certainty in their heart that "I mattered to them."

That imprint is created in the small, repeated choices:

The pause to truly listen when they speak.
The hug that lingers a second longer.
The "just checking in" call on an ordinary Tuesday.
The forgiveness offered when it's hard.
The celebration shared when they succeed.

These are the things that echo long after the money is spent, the houses are sold, and the titles are forgotten.
They are what children tell their own children, what friends carry in quiet moments, what partners hold close when the nights feel long.
That is the legacy that endures.

**Something I've Learned:**

Financial security matters, it gives freedom.
But emotional security matters more.
The legacy that endures is the feeling you leave in hearts, not the balance in accounts or material possessions.

**Story:**

My uncle was a man who built a life of considerable success. He worked tirelessly for decades, often long hours that left little time for family, invested wisely, and left behind a substantial estate: property, savings, investments that would provide for his family for years. When he passed, the family gathered, and the conversations turned quickly to the practical: dividing assets, handling the will, managing the money.
There were no tears for the man himself, only discussions of what he left behind financially.

It was sobering to witness.
The wealth was real, but the connection was thin.
His family mourned the loss of security more than the loss of him.

My dad, on the other hand, had enough to live comfortably.
He drove the same old truck for decades, paid every bill on time, and had everything that he needed.
But when he passed, the family didn't gather to talk about accounts or assets.
Instead, we gathered to share stories: his late-night calls just to say hi, the way he showed up for me burnt toast and all, through every ordinary, imperfect moment.
We laughed until we cried remembering his worried pacing when something needed fixing, his quiet strength when life was hard, his lingering hugs that made everything feel safe.
We didn't mourn possessions.
We mourned the man, the love he gave in steady, everyday ways.

Years later, those memories are what we hold close.
They are what my children share with their own kids.
They are the warmth that fills the room when we talk about him.

Money buys things that fade.
Love buys memories that echo forever.

**Reflection Prompt:**

If money vanished tomorrow, what would your legacy be?
How can you strengthen it today?

**Challenge 6:**

This week, replace one "productivity" hour with a connection hour.
Call a friend. Play with your kids. Or sit quietly with your spouse (or anyone you love), no conversation required, just shared presence.

Feel the shift: love is sometimes spoken, sometimes played, and sometimes simply felt in the gentle silence together. Love always wins.

## Bonus: Legacy Reflection Questions

Open your favorite journal or notebook and let these questions gently guide you. Return to this page every few months. Your legacy is always unfolding, and each reflection reveals just how beautifully it continues to grow.

1. Who in my life already makes me feel truly valued?
   How do they do it?

2. What small tradition from my past do I cherish?
   How can I bring it back or adapt it today?

3. If tomorrow was my last day, what would people say about how I made them feel?
4. Who might need to hear from me right now that they matter?

5. What everyday habit could I start to make someone feel more seen and cherished?

6. How has grief or loss shaped the way I love today?

7. What one change would deepen my relationships most right now?

8. Who do I want to write a "Why You Matter" letter to?

9. How can I be more present in my daily life?

10. What legacy of love am I already building and how can I make

it even brighter?

# CHAPTER 7: INTEGRITY IN LOVE - BEING HONEST AND TRUE

Love without integrity is like a house built on sand. It may look beautiful for a while, but when the storms come, it crumbles.

Integrity is the steady foundation beneath every lasting relationship.
It's not about being perfect; it's about being real, reliable, and respectful, even when it's uncomfortable.
Integrity shows up in the small, everyday choices that build trust over time, and it protects love when life gets hard.

Integrity looks like this:

- Admitting when you're wrong, without defensiveness or excuses.
  A simple "I'm sorry. I messed up" spoken with humility can heal more than any elaborate justification ever could.
- Keeping promises, both big and small.
  When you say you'll be there, you show up. When you promise to call, you call. These quiet follow-throughs whisper, "You can count on me."
- Showing up as your real self, vulnerabilities included.
  Hiding parts of who you are might feel safe in the moment, but it creates distance. Letting someone see your doubts, your fears, your imperfections invites them to do the same, and that's where true closeness begins.

- Speaking truth kindly, even when it's hard.
  Honesty without kindness can wound. Kindness without honesty can mislead. Integrity finds the gentle middle ground: truth wrapped in care, delivered with respect.

When these qualities are present, love feels safe.

Trust grows deep roots.
People can relax, knowing they won't be judged harshly, abandoned quietly, or misled gently.
They feel secure enough to be fully themselves, and that security becomes the soil where love flourishes for years.

**Something I've Learned:**

Integrity is the quiet strength that holds love steady through every season.
It's not flashy or dramatic, it's the daily practice of being honest, reliable, and fully present, even when it's uncomfortable.

When integrity is alive, love doesn't just survive; it deepens, grows deep roots, weathers any storm, and becomes something that truly lasts.

**Story:**

Years ago, my husband and I hit a rough patch.
Nothing dramatic, just the slow buildup of unspoken frustrations, missed expectations, and the quiet drift that can happen when life gets busy.
One evening, after the kids were in bed, I finally said it: "I've been feeling like we're not really connecting lately, and I'm scared we're losing something important."
I braced for defensiveness, for explanations, for the usual dance of "but you..."
Instead, he took a slow breath, looked me in the eyes, and said,

"You're right. I've been distracted, and I haven't been showing up the way I want to. I'm sorry. I want to fix this with you."

No excuses. No counter-arguments.
Just honesty, humility, and the promise to try again.

That single moment of integrity, of owning his part without blame, changed everything. It opened the door to real conversation, to healing, to rebuilding.

We didn't fix it overnight, but we started moving toward each other again.
And because he chose honesty over protection, I felt safe to do the same.
It took courage from both of us: his willingness to own his part fully, and my willingness to speak the hard truth with candor and care.
That "art of candor with care" from both sides became one of the strongest threads in our marriage.
It's not the loud, romantic gestures we remember most.
It's the times we were brave enough to be real, to say the hard thing with kindness, and to show up again and again.

**Reflection Prompt:**

Pause and look gently at your relationships:

- Where have you been fully honest lately?
- Where might you have held back a truth, softened an apology, or avoided a hard conversation?
- What would change if you chose integrity in one small way this week, speaking kindly, keeping a promise, showing up as your real self?

**Challenge 7:**

This week, practice one act of integrity in a relationship that matters to you. It could be:

- Admitting a mistake without excuses ("l was wrong, and I'm sorry").
- Keeping a promise you've made, even if it's small.
- Sharing a vulnerable truth you've been holding back ("This has been hard for me...").
- Speaking a difficult truth with kindness and care.

Do it with gentleness toward yourself and the other person. Notice how it feels both in the moment and afterward.

That single choice is building the foundation of a love that lasts.

# CHAPTER 8: HEALING BROKEN RELATIONSHIPS BEFORE IT'S TOO LATE

Few things weigh heavier at the end of life than the quiet ache of unfinished business with the people we once loved or still do.
A grudge held too long, a sharp word that was never softened, a misunderstanding that grew into silence, a door we closed and never reopened.

These are the regrets that surface in the stillness of late nights, the ones that whisper, "I wish I'd said something sooner."
We tell ourselves there's time.
We convince ourselves the rift is too wide, the hurt too deep, or the pride too stubborn to bend.
But time is the one thing we can never reclaim.

Every day we wait, the bridge grows a little weaker, the distance a little colder, and the possibility of reconnection slips further away.

Yet here's the gentle truth: healing broken relationships doesn't require perfection, grand apologies, or mutual agreement.
It doesn't demand that both sides see the story the same way.

What it does require is something simpler, though often harder courage and compassion.
The courage to reach out first, to risk rejection or awkwardness,

and the compassion to listen without defending, to see the other person's pain without needing to erase your own.
Forgiving doesn't mean forgetting.

It doesn't mean excusing what happened.
It means choosing to release the weight you've carried so you can walk forward lighter, freer to love again, whether that love is restored in full, or simply acknowledged in peace.

**Something I've Learned:**

Reconciliation doesn't require agreement.
It requires courage and compassion.
Forgiving doesn't mean forgetting; it means freeing yourself to love again, whether in full restoration or in peaceful farewell.

**Story:**

My cousin Sarah and her mom hadn't spoken in almost eight years.
It started over something small, a misunderstanding about family money during a difficult time, but it snowballed into accusations, hurt feelings, and eventually total silence.
Christmas cards stopped. Phone numbers were deleted.

Holidays were spent in separate homes of the same town. Both women felt justified, both felt wounded, and both quietly believed the other should make the first move.
Then came the diagnosis.

Sarah's mom, my Aunt Linda, had aggressive cancer and the doctors didn't offer much hope. Sarah heard the news through a family member and felt the ground shift beneath her.

All those years of stubborn silence suddenly felt unbearable.
She drove to the hospital the next day, hands shaking, heart pounding.
When she walked into the room, her mom looked up from the

bed, eyes wide with surprise.
Sarah didn't have a script.
She just said, "l miss you. I'm sorry for my part in this. I don't want to lose any more time."
There were tears.
There were words that had waited years to be spoken.
There was no instant fix, no magic erasure of the past, but there was honesty, there was presence.

For the next six months, they rebuilt what they could.
They talked, they laughed, they cried, they sat in silence together.
Sarah held her mom's hand when the pain was too much.
They shared memories, old photos, even apologies that came too late for perfection but arrived right on time for healing.

When Aunt Linda passed, Sarah didn't have to carry the weight of "what if I'd reached out sooner?"
She had the gift of those six months, and that gift became part of her own legacy: the courage to choose love over pride.

That story reminds me that reconciliation isn't about winning an argument or proving who was right.
It's about choosing connection over separation, even when it's messy, even when it's late.
Sometimes the bridge becomes strong again, ready to bear the weight of new days together.
Sometimes it holds only long enough for one final, precious crossing.
In either case, the simple act of reaching out first is a quiet, courageous gift of love. It says, in the most human way possible, “You mattered so much to me that I couldn’t let silence be the last word.”
And that moment of choosing connection, no matter how late or imperfect, is something we carry with us forever.

**Reflection Prompt:**

Who do you need to heal with?
What person (or relationship) do you need to heal from?
Who in your life carries unfinished business with you?
What small step could you take this week, a call, a message, a handwritten note, or simply showing up?
What's the one thing you'd most regret never saying?

**Challenge 8:**

Reach out to someone you've drifted from or hurt.
Keep it simple and honest: "I miss you. Can we talk?" or "I've been thinking about us, and I'd like to clear the air if you're open to it."
No expectations. No need to win.
Just open the door.
The attempt alone is part of the legacy you're building, one of love that refuses to let silence win.

# CHAPTER 9: CREATING FAMILY TRADITIONS THAT LAST GENERATIONS

Traditions are the quiet glue of legacy.

They give a family its own rhythm, its own heartbeat.

They say, without ever needing to be spoken aloud, "This is who we are.
This is what matters to us."

They don't have to be elaborate or expensive.
The most powerful ones are often the simplest.
Sunday morning pancake breakfasts where the kitchen smells like butter and laughter, the annual trip to the same little beach where everyone still fights over the best towel spot, or the way you always watch the same holiday movie together even though everyone knows the lines by heart.
These rituals become anchors.
In a world that changes constantly, they offer something steady: belonging, continuity, and the unspoken promise that "you are part of us, and we are part of you."

What makes traditions so enduring is that they create shared memory.
They give children stories to tell their own children.
They give adults moments to look back on when life feels fragmented.

Most importantly, they make every person in the circle feel valued because they're included, because they're expected, and because they're needed for the tradition to feel complete.

**Something I've Learned:**

Simple rituals create a sense of belonging that can survive decades, even generations. They don't require perfection or grand scale, just consistency and love.
When someone is part of a family tradition, they feel chosen, seen, and cherished in a way that words alone can't convey.

**Story:**

It began in the 1950s with my grandparents, when the house was small, money was tight, and evenings were simple.

Every Friday evening, after dinner, everyone gathered in the living room, kids cross-legged on the floor, adults sinking into worn couches and one by one, they shared a story from the week.
It could be funny (the time Grandpa locked himself out of the car in his pajamas), tender (how Grandma felt proud when my mom stood up for a friend at school), or perfectly ordinary (the silly thing the dog did in the yard).
There were no rules except honesty and kindness. No judgment, no need for polish, just the warmth of being heard.

My grandparents passed the habit to my parents, who kept it alive through busy workweeks and growing kids.

When my husband and I started our own family, we carried it forward without question.
Our children grew up in that circle, learning to share their own stories, about school plays, playground adventures, or the time they "helped" bake cookies and ended up covered in flour from head to toe.

Now, those children are grown, with homes and families of their own.
Yet the tradition lives on.
Every Friday evening, they gather their young children, the next generation, around their own living rooms, continuing the same simple practice: sharing stories from the week, laughing, listening, and letting each voice matter.
The room still carries the faint scent of coffee and cinnamon, just as it always has.
It's not fancy.
We don't dress up or light candles.
There are no elaborate props or perfect lighting.
But it's ours, handed down like a treasured heirloom, one story at a time.
Every time we gather, I see it in their eyes: the quiet certainty that they belong here, that their voice matters, that this space will always be waiting for them, no matter how far life takes them.

That's the true power of tradition: it turns ordinary moments into something sacred, weaving love and belonging through decades, through generations, until the very act of gathering becomes a legacy in itself.

**Reflection Prompt:**

Think back: What tradition from your childhood or past still warms your heart when you remember it?
Why did it feel special?
How could you adapt or recreate it today, in your own family, with friends, or with chosen loved ones?
What small ritual could you begin that would say, "This is who we are, and you're part of it"?

**Challenge 9:**

Start or revive one family tradition this month.
Keep it simple and realistic, something you can do consistently without stress.
Involve the next generation early: let them help plan, participate, or even lead parts of it.
Teach them (and remind yourself) that it's not about perfection, burnt pancakes, rainy beach days, or silly stories are all part of the magic.
It's about love, inclusion, and the promise that "this will always be here for you."
The moment you begin, you start planting something that may outlive you.

Traditions aren't about impressing anyone.
They're about belonging.
They're about saying, through repetition and care, "You are part of something bigger than yourself, and we're so glad you're here."

That is a legacy worth building, one Friday night, one Sunday breakfast, one beach trip at a time.

## Bonus: Tradition Planner

Open your favorite journal or notebook and use this template to thoughtfully plan and track a new or revived family tradition. These small, intentional moments have a way of becoming the heart of your family's story.

- Name we are giving our tradition:

- Frequency (e.g., weekly, monthly, yearly):

- Who will participate:
- Why it matters (how it shows love, belonging, or connection:
- First date to try:
- What we need to make it happen (supplies, time, location:
- How we'll make it flexible and fun (so it's not stressful:
- Notes after first try (what worked, what to change:
- Date to try again:

## Bonus: Discovering Our Family Values Through Stories

This worksheet helps families identify core shared values and link them to personal stories, creating a foundation for traditions, conversations, and legacies. It's perfect for multi-generational use. Parents/grandparents can complete it first, then involve children to spark meaningful discussions.

**Guidance for this page:**

Choose a peaceful time, like a cozy evening or weekend, to reflect together or on your own. Gather as a family to share memories and values openly, or give each person their own sheet of paper or notebook for individual reflection. Let it unfold naturally, without hurry, as you capture what truly matters in your family.

**Section 1: Our Core Family Values:**

**Value-**

List 5-7 values that define how your family shows love, support, and kindness.

- Examples: kindness, resilience, humor, generosity, honesty, adventure, faith.

**Why This Value?-**

This invites you to reflect on how and where it has shown up in your lives (e.g., from personal experiences, cultural background, hardships overcome, or joyful moments).

**Examples:**

- Kindness-"Because we've seen how one small act can turn around a tough day for someone we love, and it makes us feel more connected."
- Resilience-"It carried us through Grandma's illness last year. We kept showing up for each other, and it strengthened out bond."
- Honesty- "Growing up, I learned that trust is fragile; being truthful has always kept our family close and safe."
- Humor- "We laughed every time Mom tried to "help" Dad with the grill, mostly because the burgers ended up looking like hockey pucks. But somehow, those charred patties always

tasted better when we ate them together, arguing over who got the extra bun."

1. Value:
   Why this value?

2. Value:
   Why this value?

3. Value:
   Why this value?

4. Value:
   Why this value?

5. Value:
   Why this value?

6. Value:
   Why this value?

7. Value:
   Why this value?

**Section 2: Stories That Embody These Values:**

For each value from Section 1 (or pick your top 3), write a short family story or memory that shows it in action. Include who was involved, what happened, and how it made everyone feel.

Value 1:
Story:
Feelings it created:

Value 2:
Story:
Feelings it created:

Value 3:
Story:
Feelings it created:

Value 4:
Story:
Feelings it created:

Value 5:
Story:
Feelings it created:

Value 6:
Story:
Feelings it created:

Value 7:
Story:
Feelings it created:

**Section 3: How We Can Live These Values Today:**

Choose one value and one small way to practice it this week (e.g., a daily act of kindness, sharing a laugh, or helping without being asked).

Value chosen:
Action plan:
Who will join me?

**Closing Reflection Prompt:**

What surprised you most about what came up?

How does naming these values and stories make you feel more connected to your loved ones?

Revisit this worksheet every 6-12 months. Values evolve, and new stories add richness to your legacy of love.

# CHAPTER 10: THE COST OF NOT BEING PRESENT

When we're distracted by phones, work, and endless worries, we miss the moments that matter most. The price we pay? Regret. Loneliness. Bonds that quietly weaken over time.

We live in a world designed to pull our attention in a thousand directions at once. Phones buzz with notifications, work emails demand instant replies, worries whisper in the back of our minds, and to-do lists stretch longer than the day.
In the rush to stay on top of everything, we often miss the one thing that truly matters, the people right in front of us.
The moments slip by unnoticed: the way your child's eyes light up when they tell you about their day, the quiet sigh your spouse lets out after a long one, the small smile your parent gives when you walk into the room.
We think we'll catch them later.
We tell ourselves there's always tomorrow.
But tomorrow has a way of becoming yesterday, and those little moments don't wait.
The cost of distraction is subtle at first.
A missed laugh here, a half-listened story there.
Over time, though, the price becomes heavier: regret that settles in like fog, loneliness that grows in the spaces we leave empty, bonds that quietly weaken until they feel thin and fragile.
We end up with people we love living under the same roof, yet

miles apart in every way that counts.

The deepest truth is this: absence costs more than presence ever will.
Loneliness doesn't grow in the quiet; it grows in the gaps we leave when we're physically there but emotionally gone.
Presence fills those gaps with love.
It says, without a single word, "You are worth my full attention. You matter more than the next ping on my screen."

**Something I've Learned:**

Absence costs more than presence ever will.
Loneliness grows in the gaps we leave but presence fills them with love, trust, and the deep knowing that "I am important to you."

**Story:**

I think of a colleague I worked with for years.
He was brilliant, driven, always chasing the next promotion, the next deadline, the next milestone.
He told himself he was building security for his family, better schools, bigger house, college funds.
But his kids grew up fast.
He missed soccer games, school plays, quiet evenings when they just wanted to talk. He was at the office when his daughter learned to ride a bike, and he was on a conference call when his son scored his first goal.

When retirement finally came, he sat in his new home office, surrounded by awards and savings statements, and said something I'll never forget: "I have the money now, but I lost the time. They're grown, and I barely know the people they've become."
His voice cracked as he said it.
The regret was real, raw, and irreversible.
He wasn't mourning the lack of wealth, he was mourning the

lack of presence.

Don't let that be your story.
The good news is that presence is a choice we can make every single day.
It doesn't require hours we don't have.
It requires intention.
A few minutes of undivided attention can heal more than a lifetime of half-hearted "I'm listening" ever could.
When we put the phone down, close the laptop, silence the inner noise, and simply show up, fully, quietly, completely, we give the gift of being seen.
And that gift echoes in ways money never can.

**Reflection Prompt:**

Pause and look honestly at your week:
Where is distraction stealing your presence?
Is work bleeding into family time?
Screens pulling you away during conversations?
Worry keeping your mind elsewhere even when you're in the same room?
Name one person who might be feeling the absence most.
What would change if you gave them your full attention, even just for a little while?

**Challenge 10:**

This week, replace one "productivity" hour with a true connection hour.
Turn off notifications, set the phone aside, and be fully present with someone you love.
Call a friend and listen without multitasking.
Play with your grandkids and let the game be the only thing that matters.

Simply sit with your spouse in comfortable silence, no conversation required, just shared presence, breathing the same air, feeling the warmth of being together.

Notice the difference: deeper talks when words come, more laughter, quieter comfort, real connection.

Feel the shift: from doing to being, from distraction to love.

That single hour can become the memory that matters most.

# CHAPTER 11: DIGITAL LEGACY - PRESERVING YOUR LOVE ONLINE

Much of our life now lives in the digital world.
Photos we snap on our phones, text messages that carry quick "thinking of you" notes, videos of first steps or last birthdays, emails that once held everyday check-ins, social media posts that captured moments we wanted to remember.
These fragments are no longer just files.
They are pieces of our story, echoes of our voice, traces of our love.

When we're no longer here, they become part of what our loved ones hold onto.
Your digital footprint is not separate from your legacy; it is woven into it.
The same way a handwritten letter or a faded photo album once passed memories from one generation to the next, today's digital traces do the same, only faster, more widely, and sometimes more vulnerably.
Left unmanaged, they can become cluttered noise or, worse, sources of pain.
Curated with intention, they become treasures that heal, comfort, and keep love alive long after the last goodbye.

The truth is simple but profound: digital memories can heal or

hurt.
A gallery full of joyful photos can bring smiles on hard days; a harsh comment left online can reopen old wounds years later.
An unorganized cloud drive might leave your family searching for hours, overwhelmed by thousands of files.

But a thoughtfully organized collection, carefully saved, lovingly labeled, gently shared, can feel like you're still in the room, still speaking, still loving them through the screen.

**Something I've Learned:**

Digital memories are powerful extensions of your presence.
They can preserve the sound of your laugh, the warmth of your words, the proof of your care.
Choose to curate them with the same love you give in person: save what uplifts, gently release what no longer serves, and make sure the people you love know how to find the good pieces when they need them most.

**Story:**

My dad's dementia had taken so much from him, his ability to walk, to spell, to read, even to feed himself without help.
We lived in a quiet, aching awareness that our time with him was slipping away, each day a fragile gift.

One afternoon, when the light was gentle and he was having one of his rare "good days," I felt a sudden, gentle pull to capture something, anything, of him while I still could.
I pulled out my phone, sat close beside him, and simply started recording.
I didn't script it. I just said, "Dad, say anything you want to say."
His eyes, cloudy as they were, found mine for a moment, and then something beautiful happened.
My dad, who hadn't remembered my puppy's name in months,

couldn't recall so many things, looked straight into the camera and spoke to my little dog.
His voice, thin but steady, carried the same familiar warmth I'd known all my life.
"Be a good boy for mommy" he said slowly, clearly, lovingly. "Listen to her. Take care of her for me."
He even said the puppy's name, perfectly, like it had never been lost.
I sat there, tears streaming, holding the phone with trembling hands, watching him pour every remaining bit of his heart into that message.
That short video, barely a minute long, is the only recording I have of his voice.
I watch it on the hardest days, when the silence feels too loud, and I hear him still speaking love into the world.

I wish I had more, more moments captured, more of his voice, more of him, but I treasure this one fiercely.
It reminds me that even when everything else fades, love finds a way to stay, clear and unbroken, forever.

**Reflection Prompt:**

Pause for a moment and think about your own digital life.
What photos, videos, messages, or posts would bring comfort to your loved ones on a difficult day?
What might cause confusion, pain, or overwhelm if left untouched?
Who in your life would you trust to help preserve the beautiful parts?
What one small step could you take this week to start curating your digital legacy with love?

**Challenge 11:**

Create a shared family photo album, digital memory box, or private folder that will live on for your loved ones.

Choose a platform that feels simple and secure, Google Photos shared album, Apple Shared Albums, a password-protected cloud drive, or even a dedicated external hard drive.
Start small: add one meaningful memory each week, a photo from a family dinner, a screenshot of a sweet text, a voice recording of you saying "I love you" or telling a favorite story, a short video of laughter or a quiet moment together, or an old email that still makes you smile.
Label them with dates and a few words of context ("Emma's first laugh," "Grandpa's favorite fishing spot," "Mom's goodnight voice message," "The day we all got caught in the rain").
When it feels ready, share access with trusted loved ones, give them the password, the link, the instructions.
Tell them why: "These are the pieces of us I want you to have, whenever you need a reminder that you were loved. Play my voice when you miss me. Watch our videos when you need a laugh."

This is not about creating a perfect archive.
It's about leaving breadcrumbs of love, small, honest, everyday reminders that you were here, that you thought of them, that they mattered.

In the quiet moments after you're gone, those digital traces can become voices again. They can bring back your laugh, your words, your gentle "I'm proud of you," the sound of your breathing as you watched your grandchildren play.
They can remind your family that even in absence, love doesn't disappear, it simply changes form.
And that is one of the most beautiful ways to keep your legacy alive.

# CHAPTER 12: WRITE YOUR OWN "WHY YOU MATTER" LETTERS

There is something almost sacred about words written on paper, or even typed with care and printed out.
They slow us down.
They force us to choose each one deliberately.
And when those words say, "You matter to me because...," they become a gift that can outlive us.
A "Why You Matter" letter is a deeply personal gift that lasts.
It's not a generic greeting card message or a fleeting compliment.
It's specific, honest, and straight from your heart, naming exactly why this person is irreplaceable to you: the way their presence calms you, the quiet strength they carry, the little things they do that make your days brighter.
When someone receives those words on paper, they hold something real and lasting in their hands.
In moments of doubt, loneliness, or simply a hard day, they can unfold it, read it again, trace the lines with their fingers, and feel the warmth of your voice in every sentence: "I am seen. I am cherished. I truly matter to someone."

That's the quiet power of putting love into writing, it becomes a keepsake they can return to whenever they need to feel that connection again, a gentle reminder of the love that's always been there.
These letters become treasures.
They're tucked into wallets, folded into books, slipped into mem-

ory boxes.
They're read on birthdays, anniversaries, or ordinary Tuesdays when the world feels heavy.

Spoken words can fade from memory; written words endure.
They carry weight long after the moment they were given, becoming quiet companions that speak love when we can no longer do it ourselves.

**Something I've Learned:**

Written words carry weight long after spoken words fade.
They become anchors, quiet proof that someone was truly seen, cherished, and valued. A single letter can become a lifeline, a gentle reminder that love was real and intentional, even when everything else feels uncertain.

**Story:**

My husband and I have been married for nearly thirty years, and through every season, busy parenting years, quiet empty-nest days, celebrations, and ordinary routines, he has quietly given me the most beautiful gift: little love letters.
They never come on fancy stationery.
Sometimes he writes them on the back of a Christmas notepad in the middle of July, on a paper napkin from the kitchen table, on the corner of a grocery list, or even on the back of an old receipt.
The paper is always whatever is closest, as if the feeling was too urgent to wait for the "right" thing.

But the words... oh, the words.
"You make every room brighter just by walking in."
"I still can't believe I get to wake up next to you every day."
"Thank you for loving me when I'm not easy to love."
"I'm proud of the woman you are today, the mother you were to our children, and the grandmother you've become to our

grandchildren. You've always been, and still are, such a beautiful friend, too."
Some are short, just a sentence or two.
Others spill across the page, telling me exactly why I matter to him in that particular moment.

He never makes a big production of it.
He just leaves them where I'll find them: tucked under my coffee mug, slipped into my book, folded inside my purse.
Over the years, I've saved every single one.
They live in a small, worn wooden box on my dresser, hundreds of little scraps of paper, each one a heartbeat of his love.
I open that box on hard days, when doubt creeps in or life feels heavy, and I read them again.
Each note reminds me: I am seen. I am cherished. I am valued.

I've told him I want that box passed down to our children and grandchildren one day.
Not because the papers are valuable in any material way, but because they are proof of love in action, proof that love can be simple, spontaneous, imperfect, and still last a lifetime.
When I'm gone, I want them to read those notes and feel the warmth of a marriage built on quiet, everyday affirmations.
I want them to understand that real love doesn't require big moments; it shines brightest in the small, honest ones spoken from the heart or written and saved to hold onto forever.

That little box is one of the most precious parts of the legacy we're building together. And every time he hands me another napkin note or Christmas-card scrap, I'm reminded: the smallest written word can become the loudest echo of love.

**Reflection Prompt:**

Pause and think about the people in your life right now.
Who might need to hear, in your own words, "You matter to me

because..."?
A spouse? A child? A sibling? A friend who's been there through everything?
What specific qualities, memories, or actions make them irreplaceable to you? What would change for them, and for you, if they knew exactly how deeply you value them?

**Challenge 12:**

Write one "Why You Matter" letter this week.
Be specific. Be honest. Let your words come from the heart.
Tell them why they matter: the way they make you laugh, the strength they show, the small things they do that no one else notices.
Seal it in an envelope (or print it if you typed it).
Give it when the moment feels right, hand it to them over coffee, slip it into their bag, mail it across town. Or save it for a milestone, a birthday, anniversary, or simply a day they might need it most.
This small act takes only minutes, but the ripple can last a lifetime.
You are giving someone proof that they are seen, cherished, and valued, tangible, lasting proof they can hold in their hands when doubt creeps in.
That is one of the most beautiful gifts you can ever give, and one of the most enduring pieces of the legacy you're building.

# CHAPTER 13: WHEN GRIEF COMES-HOW LOVE CARRIES YOU THROUGH

Grief is one of life's most tender, unraveling experiences. It arrives uninvited, heavy and raw, like a storm that steals the breath from your chest and the light from your days.

It's love with nowhere to go, love that once flowed freely in hugs, conversations, and shared moments, now left aching in the silence of absence.

But here's the gentle truth that grief teaches us, if we let it: love doesn't end with loss.

It simply changes form.

The love you've built, the calls, the laughs, the quiet ways you showed up for each other, becomes a bridge that carries you through the darkness.

It transforms into stories you tell, memories you hold close, traditions you pass on. It lives in the way you love others now, with a little more tenderness because you know how precious it is.

Grief doesn't erase love; it reshapes it into something enduring, something that whispers, "They were here. They mattered. And so do you."

In those early, shattering days after someone we love is gone, it can feel impossible to see this.

The world feels dimmer, emptier, forever altered.
But over time, as the sharp edges soften, we discover that love has a way of holding us up.
It shows up in unexpected places: a song that plays on the radio, a scent that drifts by, a habit we catch ourselves doing that reminds us of them.
And in those moments, grief and love walk hand in hand, not as enemies, but as companions on the same path.

**Something I've Learned:**

Love doesn't end with loss, it changes form, becoming the stories we tell, the memories we cherish, the traditions we carry forward.
Grief reshapes love into something that honors the person we lost while guiding us to love even more deeply in the days ahead.
It's the bridge that reminds us: what was real and beautiful once will always be real and beautiful, in whatever shape it takes.

**Story:**

When my dad's dementia deepened, we all carried the quiet weight of knowing our time with him was limited.
We cherished every clear moment, held our breath during the confusion, and tried to prepare ourselves for what was coming.
But knowing the end was near didn't soften the pain when he finally slipped away.
The loss still came like a wave, sudden and overwhelming, leaving a hollow space nothing could fill.

One memory I hold especially close happened long before the dementia took hold, when I was just twelve years old.
I was home sick from school, feverish and miserable on the couch, body aching, head pounding, everything too loud and too bright.
Dad came home from work early that day.

He didn't say much; he just looked at me with that worried, gentle expression he always had, then disappeared without a word.
About forty minutes later, the front door opened again.
He walked in carrying a familiar paper bag, the smell of french fries and cheeseburgers drifting through the house.
It was my favorite fast food from the little drive-thru down the road, the one with the crispy fries and the chocolate shake I loved.
He set it on the coffee table in front of me, sat down on the floor beside the couch so he was right at my level, and said softly, "I figured this might help you feel a little better, kiddo."
He stayed there the rest of the afternoon.
No lectures about getting back to school tomorrow, no rushing off to do chores.
He just sat with me, handing me fries one at a time when my hands were shaky, talking softly about silly things until I started to smile again.
That simple act, driving across town, picking up my favorite meal, sitting on the floor beside me when I felt small and sick, was love in its purest, quietest form: "I see you hurting. I'm here. You're worth the effort."

Years later, when dementia stole so much of him, that memory became one of the lights that carried me through the grief.
I would sit with him on his last good days, holding his hand, and I'd whisper to myself: "He showed me how to love when someone is hurting. I can still do that now, for him and for my family and for others."

I share that story with my grown children now and my grandchildren.
Woven into every family gathering are tales of Grandpa: how he worried over every problem until he solved it, how his hugs felt like home, how his love was in the small, steady ways he showed up.

My kids laugh and say, "Remember when Grandpa called just to say hi?"
And my grandchildren listen wide-eyed, absorbing him through our words.

It's in these moments that I feel his love carrying us all forward.

Grief still visits sometimes, especially on quiet afternoons or when I see something that reminds me of him, a familiar fast-food bag, a song that he loved or an old couch that looks like the one he loved to sit on with me to watch old tv shows.
But it's softer now, gentler.
It's love in a new form, stories that bridge the years, memories that keep him close, traditions that let the next generation know the man who loved so well.

My dad's love didn't end when he left us.
It lives in every call we make just to say hi, every hug that lingers a little longer, every story we share around the table.
And in sharing him with my children and grandchildren, I see his legacy unfolding, warm, steady, and full of light.

**Reflection Prompt:**

Pause for a quiet moment and reflect: How has grief shaped you? What parts of it have made you softer, stronger, or more present in your relationships?
What love from your past, words, moments, traditions, still helps you through the hard days?
Who in your life might benefit from hearing one of those stories today?
How can you keep that love alive in small ways right now?

**Challenge 13:**

Create a small, personal ritual for remembering someone you've lost, a way to honor their love and let it carry you forward.
It can be as simple as lighting a candle on their birthday or a

quiet evening, sharing one story about them with your family, or saying their name aloud with gratitude: "Thank you, Dad, for teaching me how to love."
Make it yours, something that feels warm and true.
Do it regularly, even just once a month.
Let this ritual be a bridge: a way to feel their presence, to let love flow through the pain, and to share their light with the people who are still here.

Grief will come and go, but love stays.
It carries you through, not by erasing the hurt, but by holding you steady in it.
And in that holding, you discover that the love you've built doesn't just survive loss, it becomes the very thing that helps you live more fully, love more deeply, and pass it on to those who come after you.

That's the beautiful, enduring gift of love: it never truly leaves.
It simply changes forms, carrying us all forward together.

# CHAPTER 14: THE 20 CHALLENGES: YOUR INVITATION TO LIVE LOVE EVERY DAY

You've walked through these pages reflecting on love, connection, and the quiet ways we leave a lasting legacy. Now comes the most meaningful part: bringing it all into your everyday life.

These 20 challenges are simple invitations, small, doable steps that invite you to practice love in real time.
You may recognize some ideas from earlier chapters; that's intentional.
Repetition is how love grows roots.
When we return to the same gentle habits again and again, they become part of who we are, weaving deeper into our relationships and our legacy.

There's no pressure to do them all at once, or in perfect order.

- Try one challenge per day for a month if that feels exciting.
- Or simply choose the ones that speak to you right now.
- Do them in any rhythm that feels true, once a week, twice a month, whenever your heart nudges you.

Each challenge includes a short "why it matters" note (to remind you of the deeper purpose), a starting example, and a gentle invitation to reflect.

This isn't about perfection or checking boxes.
It's about showing up, one small moment at a time, with intention and care.
These acts, however tiny, add up.
They become the stories your loved ones will carry, the warmth they'll remember, the proof that they were truly seen, cherished, and valued by you.
You're already doing so much of this.
These challenges are simply gentle reminders to keep going, to stay present, to let love lead.

Take your time. Let them unfold naturally.
Your legacy of love is already beautiful and every challenge you embrace makes it shine even brighter.

1. **Listen without fixing - make someone feel heard.**

- Why: Shows you value their voice.
- Example to get started: When your partner or child shares about a tough day, resist offering solutions right away. Instead, nod, maintain eye contact, and say, "That sounds really hard. Tell me more about how you're feeling."
- Reflection invitation: What came up for them when you truly listened? How did it feel to hold space without jumping in?

2. **Give a soul-deep compliment.**

- Why: Builds self-worth.
- Example to get started: Instead of "You look nice," try "I'm so proud of how patient you are with your little sister. It shows what a kind heart you have."

- Reflection invitation: How did they light up? What made this compliment feel deeper than surface-level?

3. **Forgive a small hurt today.**

- Why: Frees space for love.
- Example to get started: Let go of annoyance when a family member forgets to load the dishwasher. Choose a gentle reminder or simply do it with grace.
- Reflection invitation: What shifted inside you after releasing it? How might holding onto it have affected your connection?

4. **Share a family story.**

- Why: Connects generations.
- Example to get started: Over dinner, tell a funny or touching memory from your childhood, like "Remember when Grandma taught me to bake her famous cookies? Here's how it went..."
- Reflection invitation: What emotions arose as you shared? How did it make your loved ones feel closer to the past?

5. **Do something kind for someone without expecting anything in return.**

- Why: Models kindness.
- Example to get started: Surprise a neighbor with a homemade treat or help a sibling with a chore they dread. No strings attached.
- Reflection invitation: How did giving freely feel? Did it spark any unexpected warmth in return?

6. **Write three "You matter because..." notes.**

- Why: Creates tangible value.
- Example to get started: Slip notes into lunchboxes or pockets: "You matter because your laugh lights up the whole room."
- Reflection invitation: Where did you leave the notes, and how do you imagine they were received?

7. **Practice empathy first.**

- Why: Deepens understanding.
- Example to get started: When a teenager slams the door after school and snaps at you, instead of reacting with frustration, pause and gently say, "It looks like something really tough happened today. Want to talk about what's going on?"
- Reflection invitation: How did leading with empathy shift the moment for both of you? What did you learn about their inner world?

8. **Keep every promise this week.**

- Why: Builds trust.
- Example to get started: If you told your young child you'd read an extra story at bedtime tonight (even though you're exhausted), honor it. Cuddle up, read slowly, and make it special. Or if you promised a friend you'd call on Thursday, set a reminder and follow through.
- Reflection invitation: How did following through, even when it wasn't convenient, strengthen the trust between you? What small feeling of security did it create?

9. **Celebrate someone else's win loudly.**

- Why: Shows shared joy.

- Example to get started: Cheer extra enthusiastically for a child's good grade or a friend's promotion. Dance, hug, make it big!
- Reflection invitation: How did your genuine excitement multiply their happiness?

10. **Reflect nightly: "Did I make someone feel valued?"**

- Why: Builds self-awareness.
- Example to get started: In your journal or quietly in bed, note one moment (e.g., "I smiled and said thank you when they helped with dishes").
- Reflection invitation: What small act stood out? What might you add tomorrow?

11. **Give a 20-second hug.**

- Why: Releases bonding hormones.
- Example to get started: Wrap your arms around a loved one for a full 20 seconds. No quick pat. Perhaps at bedtime or goodbye.
- Reflection invitation: Did you notice any shift in how close you felt afterward?

12. **Make a "just calling to say hi" call.**

- Why: Fights isolation.
- Example to get started: Call a parent, sibling, or friend for no reason other than "I was thinking of you. How's your day going?"
- Reflection invitation: How did the simple check-in brighten their moment, and yours?

13. **Admit one mistake openly.**

- Why: Models humility.
- Example to get started: Say, "I'm sorry I snapped earlier. That wasn't fair, and I'll work on it."
- Reflection invitation: What opened up after your honesty?

14. **Start one new family tradition.**

- Why: Creates lasting bonds.
- Example to get started: Begin Sunday pancake mornings or a weekly gratitude circle before bed.
- Reflection invitation: How does this new ritual feel? What memories might it build over time?

15. **Choose presence over productivity once a day.**

- Why: Prioritizes people.
- Example to get started: Put your phone away during dinner and fully listen to the conversation.
- Reflection invitation: What did you notice when you were truly present?

16. **Express gratitude in writing.**

- Why: Amplifies positive feeling
- Example to get started: Leave a sticky note: "Thank you for always making coffee. It starts my day with love."
- Reflection invitation: How did writing it make the gratitude feel even stronger?

17. **Ask "How can I support you?" genuinely.**

- Why: Shows care.
- Example to get started: When someone seems overwhelmed, offer, "What would help you most right now?"
- Reflection invitation: What support did they need, and how did offering it feel?

18. **Share one vulnerability.**

- Why: Invites closeness.
- Example to get started: Say, "I've been feeling a little anxious lately. Talking about it helps."
- Reflection invitation: How did opening up change the dynamic?

19. **Teach kindness by living it.**

- Why: Inspires the next generation.
- Example to get started: While waiting in line at the grocery store with your grandchildren or children, quietly let someone with fewer items go ahead of you- smile warmly, step aside naturally, and continue on.
- Reflection invitation: What did you notice in your loved one's face or behavior as they watched? How might that silent moment have quietly shaped their understanding of kindness?

20. **End every day with "I love you" - mean it.**

- Why: Seals the day with love.
- Example to get started: Look them in the eyes, say it slowly, and add a quick reason: "l love you for how hard you tried today."
- Reflection invitation: How did ending with those words

wrap up the day differently?

## Bonus: Daily Reflection Journal

This template is designed to spark deeper thoughts in your daily reflection. Pick up your favorite journal or notebook, settle in, and pour your heart onto the pages. Follow this gentle guide to create your own daily reflection ritual.

Date:

Who did I make feel seen, cherished, or valued today?

One small act of love I did (or wish I had done):

How did it feel-for me and for them?

What moment today reminded me of love's quiet power?

One thing I'm grateful for in my relationships today:

Notes / Thoughts / Next small step:

# YOUR LEGACY LIVES ON: ONE FINAL TOAST TO YOU

You've reached the end of these pages, but the story of your love is far from over. It's already unfolding, beautifully and steadily, in the hearts of those around you.

Your legacy isn't something distant, waiting to begin when the timing feels perfect. It's already here, alive in the quiet ways you show up: the listening ear you lend, the hug that lingers, the "just checking in" call, the small moments where someone feels seen, cherished, and valued because of you.

The people in your life don't need perfection from you. They need the real you, the one who cares, who tries, who loves in the everyday ways that matter most. Every time you choose presence over distraction, honesty over silence, kindness over indifference, you are building something enduring. Those small, steady acts ripple outward, touching family, friends, and even strangers in ways you may never fully see.

Start where you are. Stay gentle with yourself. Keep showing up with an open heart.

Watch love grow, not as something you must begin, but a something you're already nurturing, already sharing, already passing forward.
Thank you for walking these pages with me.

Thank you for choosing love, every day, in all its quiet, powerful forms.

Your legacy is already beautiful, already touching lives, already living on. Keep letting it shine.

With all my heart,

*Amelia May Summers*

# ABOUT THE AUTHOR

## Amelia May Summers

Amelia May Summers draws on her background in education and family history preservation to create heartfelt resources that help families feel truly seen, cherished, and valued.

As a passionate storyteller and dedicated advocate, she weaves practical wisdom with genuine empathy to empower you in preserving legacies and nurturing deep, lasting connections.

Born and raised in New Jersey, Amelia developed a profound appreciation for family bonds from an early age. This foundation ignited in her a lifelong passion for strengthening relationships and celebrating the meaningful stories that shape who we are.

Her Books:
Burnt Toast and All...A Legacy of Everyday Love: Amelia offers tender insights and actionable guidance to help families deepen bonds, create cherished traditions, and build enduring legacies, all rooted in the quiet, imperfect moments of everyday love (burnt toast and all). These small, steady acts of presence, care, and connection create a legacy that lasts a lifetime and beyond.

Coming Soon: Amelia's eagerly awaited next guide will provide a clear, organized blueprint to document your wishes, safeguard essential personal and account information, preserve medical records, and honor precious family stories and memories.

This comprehensive, compassionate resource includes thoughtful space to record your life details and heartfelt history, empowering you to leave a complete legacy with clarity, confidence, and peace of mind.

A Bit More About Amelia A devoted wife, mother, and Oma (grandmother), Amelia lives in Pennsylvania, where she continues championing proactive family conversations and crafting resources that bring comfort and connection to families everywhere.

Ready to begin your legacy journey?
Connect with Amelia at AmeliaMaySummers@gmail.com to share your story.

www.ingramcontent.com/pod-product-compliance
Lightning Source LLC
LaVergne TN
LVHW090535110826
845146LV00003B/1116

* 9 7 9 8 9 9 4 5 6 5 0 7 0 *